JAVA PROGRAMMING

A GUIDE TO LEARN OOP IN JAVA

DAVID LIVINGSTON J

Contents

CHAPTER ONE

Introduction to Java Programming

Java is an Object Oriented programming language, which follows OO concepts strictly for the development of its program. In Java, even a simple program like the one that displays the message "Hello, World!" would require a class, an object-oriented element. Every program in Java starts with the word 'class'.

Without using the basic OO concepts (Class and Object), it is not possible to write a program in Java. The following is a simple "Hello, World!" program in Java:

1. class Example{
2. public static void main(String args[]){
3. System.out.println("Hello, World!");
4. }
5. }

In this Java program, **Example** is the name of the program, and is defined as a class. While running this program using Java runtime system, an instance of the class Example is created and is called an Application Object. Hence, a Java program itself is an object, which will use other objects in it.

Method main() in Java:

As in the class **Example**, every java program will have a public member function named **main()**. This function is the starting point of every Java program. As soon as an application is created, the function **main()** will be called by the OS to run the program. This function must be declared as public for start up.

The function main() takes one parameter, which is an array of strings. Through this parameter, user input can be passed to main() from command-line at the time of starting the application. As the dimension of this array is not specified, any no. of strings (messages) can be passed as input to the application.

In the above example, there is only one statement written in function main() for displaying the message "Hello, World!":

System.out.println("Hello, World!");

This is an output statement using two objects: System and out. The first object 'System' refers to the computer that runs the program and the second object 'out' refers to an output device to which the message has to be sent for display. The object 'out' provides an operation (method) called println, using which the output can be displayed on the output device.

Data Types in Java:

Java is a strongly typed language. It is more strictly typed than any other OOP language. This fact is justified based on the following three facts:

1. Every variable and expression used in Java has a type. And every type is strongly defined.
2. All assignments, whether explicit or via parameter passing in method calls are checked for type compatibility.
3. There are no automatic coercion or conversions of conflicting types. All expressions and parameters are checked by Java compiler for type compatibility.

Java defines eight simple (or elementary) data types: byte, short, int, long, char, float, double and boolean. These can be put in four groups:

- **Integer** data types – which include byte, short, int and long
- **Floating**-point numbers – float and double
- **Character** and
- **Boolean**

The simple data types represent single values. We can use them for declaring ordinary variables, constructing arrays, or for defining user-defined Method main() in Java:data types like class.

The simple types are defined to have an explicit range and mathematical behavior. Because of Java's portability requirement, all data types have a strictly defined range. For instance, an int always occupies 32 bits, regardless of the particular platform. This allows programs to be written on one platform and then ported to another platform for execution without any modification of its source code.

Identifiers and Keywords in Java:

In Java, an identifier is a name given to a method, a variable, or any other user-defined item. Java is case sensitive and hence it differentiates variables using two different cases of alphabets. For instance, index21 and Index21 are two different identifiers in Java. Rules for forming an identifier are as follows:

1. Identifiers can be of any length. It can have one or more characters that include alphabet, number, underscore and dollar sign.
2. The first letter of an identifier must be an alphabet, an underscore or a dollar sign. The remaining characters may be either a letter, a digit, a dollar sign or an underscore.
3. Use lower case for naming a variable and title case for naming a class. Method names can be formed using a verb followed by a noun. In that case, verbs are written in lower case and the noun in title case.

Need for Comments:

Comment is a non-executable line of code used either at the beginning or in between other lines of code to note some remarks about the program. It may include details such as author name, date of written or modified, logic used in a block of code, etc.

CHAPTER TWO

Writing Object Oriented Program in Java

Class is the logical construct on which the Java language is built because the class defines the nature of an object. Within a class are defined data and code that acts upon that data. And hence a class can be considered as a template that defines the form of an object.

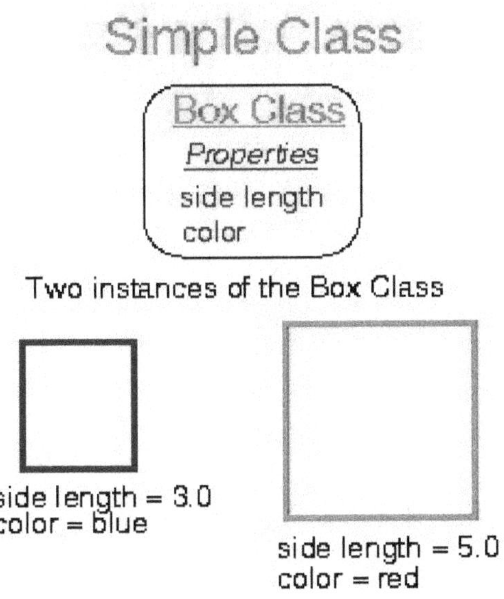

Objects are instances of a class. They are created at runtime and exist in memory during the execution of a program. Moreover, the data members associated with an object (instance of a class) are also referred to as instance variables, because memory is allocated to each and every one of them when the object is created at run time.

The Concept of Encapsulation:

Encapsulation is a programming mechanism that binds together code and data it manipulates, and that keeps both safe from outside interferene and misues. Through encapsulation, code and data can be bound together and placed in a container called **class**.

Within a class, we can declare its members - code and data. They can be declared either as private or public members. Private code or data is known to and accessible only within the object at runtime. When the members are declared public, they can be accessed from other parts of the program (i.e., outside the object). Typically, the public members act as interface to the private elements of the object.

Here is an example java program that prints the message "Hello, World!" at the time of its execution:

```
1.  class Test
2.  {
3.  public static void main(String[] args)
4.  {
5.  System.out.println("Hello, World!");
6.  }
7.  }
```

Compiling and Running a Java Program:

JDK stands for Java Development Kit, which consists of tools (also called programs) for compiling and running a Java program. **javac** and **java** are the two primary tools available in JDK. **javac**, is the compiler tool that converts java source code into byte code. Whereas, **java** is an interpreter using which we can run a byte code - compiled form of a java program. It is somethimes referred to as the application launcher. It operates on the byte code, using JVM to execute a java program.

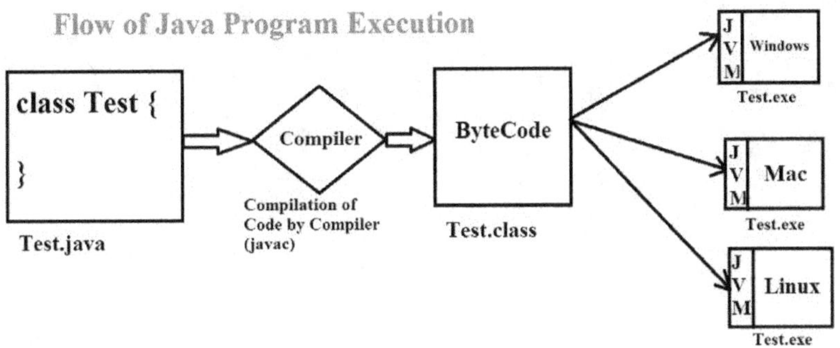

JDK tools run in a command prompt environment just like DOS commands or shell commands. The first step in creating a program in Java is to enter the source code and store it in a file with the extension .java using an editor. Then the program file must be compiled using **javac** as follows:

C:\>javac Test.java

The javac creates a file called class file (Test.class), which contains the byte code (intermediary code) equivalent of the source code available in the source file given as argument to javac. The source file (Test.java) is officially called a compilation unit. It is a text file that contsins one more more class definitions.

To actually run the program, use java tool that operatse on the byte code form of the program:

C:\\>java Test

The above java command will automatically search for a file named Test that has .class extension. If it finds the file, it will execute the code contained in the specified class.

CHAPTER THREE

Defining and Creating Objects in Java

Class is a user-defined data type in Java. It creates a new data type, from which object variables can be declared for holding the object of the new data type.

When we define a class, we declare its exact form and nature. We do this by specifying the instance variables and the methods that operate on them within the class construct.

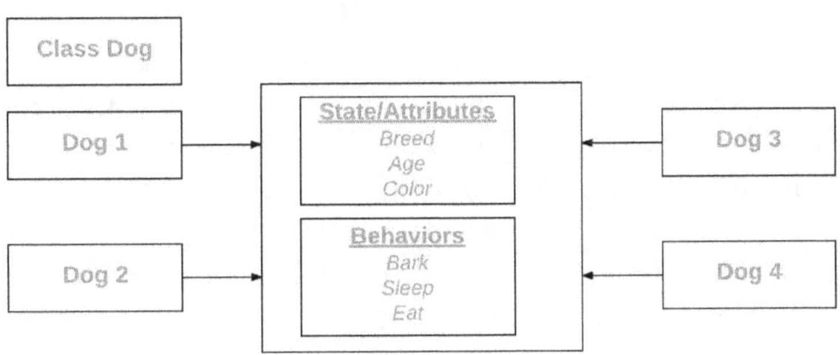

Fig. 3.1 Defining a Class of Type Dog

The methods and variables that comprise a class are called members of the class. The keyword **class** is used to define a class and its members. A simplified general form of a class definition is as follows:

```
"class classname{
    type instance-variable 1;
    type instance-variable 2;
    ..................
    ..................
    type instance-variable N;
    type method 1(parameter-list){
    //body of method
    }
    type method 2(parameter-list){
    //body of method
    }
    ..................
    ..................
    type method N(parameter-list){
    //body of method
    }
    }"
```

Class contains both variables and methods of an object. Variables determine the data to be stored in an object. The code is contained within methods. Collectively, the methods and variables defined within a class are called members of the class.

The variables of a class are called instance variables, because each instance of the class (i.e., each object of the class) contains its own copy of these variables. Thus, the data of one object are separate and unique from the data of another object.

The operations to be performed by an object are defined by the methods of the class. In Java, both declaration and definition (implementation) of the methods belong to a class are written and stored in the same place and are not separated into two. Because having specification, declaration and implementation all in one place makes for code that is easier to maintain.

Object Creation in Java:

Once an object is defined by a class, the next step involves the following two steps:

1. Declare an object variable of type class. This variable does not create the object. Instead, it is simply a variable that can refer to an object.
2. Create a physical copy of the object using the **new** keyword (also called operator) and assign its pointer to an object variable.

The first step in object creation is to declare an object variable that will hold the reference to the object to be created. Then create the new object using the class data type and the keyword - new.

The new operator dynamically allocates (i.e., allocates memory at runtime) memory for an object and returns a reference to the newly created object. The reference is, essentially the address in memory of the objected created by new. This reference is then stored in a varibale.

The syntax for declaring and creating an object in Java is as follows:

"class class-name
{
// members of the class
}
class-name obj_variable = new class-name;"

An example for the process mentioned above is as follows:

1. class Box
2. {
3. double width;
4. double height;

5. double depth;
6. }
7. Box myBox = new Box( );

In this example, Box is a new data type of type class, which contains three instance variables namely width, height, and depth. Using this data type Box, an object variable myBox is declared to hold the reference to an instance of type Box. Now the instance variables width, height, and depth of the newly created object can be accessed using myBox and a dot (.) operator:

myBox.width = 100;

Note that the object creation for myBox is done using the single statement:

Box myBox = new Box( );

This statement can be split into the following two lines of code:

Box myBox;

myBox = new Box( );

The first line declares a variable of type Box, and the second line acquires the actual, physical copy of the object and assigns it to the variable myBox. After the execution of second line, we can make use myBox as if it were a Box object.

But, in reality myBox simply holds the memory address of the actual Box object. The following figure depicts the process involved in object creation.

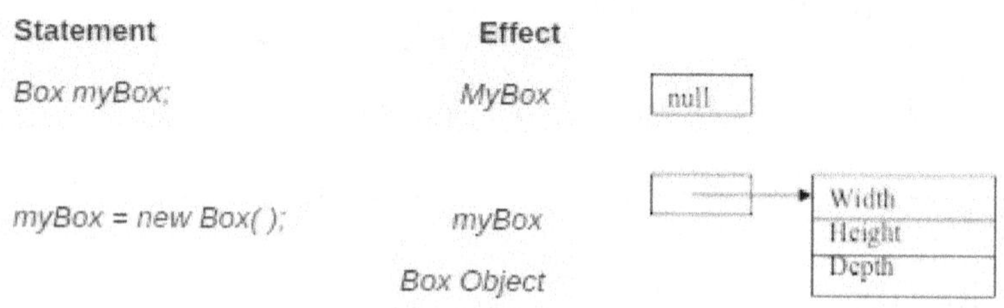

Fig. 3.2 Two Step Process of Object Creation in Java

CHAPTER FOUR

Defining Methods in a Class

Methods are subroutines that manipulate the data defined by the class, and in many cases, they control access to the data stored in an object. A method contain sthe statements that define its action. And each method performs only one task.

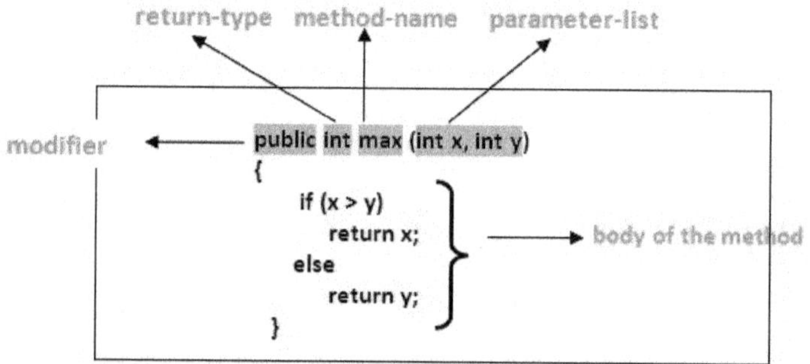

Fig. 4.1 Structure of a Method defined in a Class

Each method has a name, and it is this name that is used to call the method. A method also has a set of parantheses next to its function name and the function body enclosed in curly braces {}. The general form of the method is shown here:

> *"ret-type name(parameter-list)*
> *{*
> *// body of method*
> *}"*

Here, ret-type specifies the type of data returned by the method. This can be any valid type, including user-defined class. If the method doesn't return a value, its return type must be void.

The name is the name of the method, which must be a legal identifier other than those already used by other items within the current scope. The parameter-list is a sequence of type and identifier pairs separated by comma. Parameters are variables that receive the value of the arguments passed to the method when it is called.

Parameters Vs Arguments:

It is possible to pass one or more arguents to a method when a method is called. In method declaration, the varibale that receive the argument is called parameter. If a method takes no parameters, the parameter list will be empty.

Parameters are declared inside the paranthesis that follow the method name. The parameter declaration syntax is the same as that used for variables. A parameter has the local scope like any other local variables and acts as a placeholder for storing the value of an argument.

Constructors:

Constructors are special methods defined in a class to give initial value to the instance variables of a class. It can also be used to perform any other startup procedures required to create a fully formed object.

Generally, a constructor initializes an object when it is created. It has the same name as its class and is syntactically similar to a method. However, constructors have no explicit return type.

All classes have constructors, whether they are defined by the programmer or not. Bceause Java automatically provides a default constructor. Once a constructor is defined by the coder, the default constructor is no longer used.